The First Manifesto of Surrealism

PUBLISHER'S CHOICE

A COLLECTION OF SLIM VOLUMES
SELECTED BY OUR PUBLISHER

No. 2

FOR MARTIN CORKE

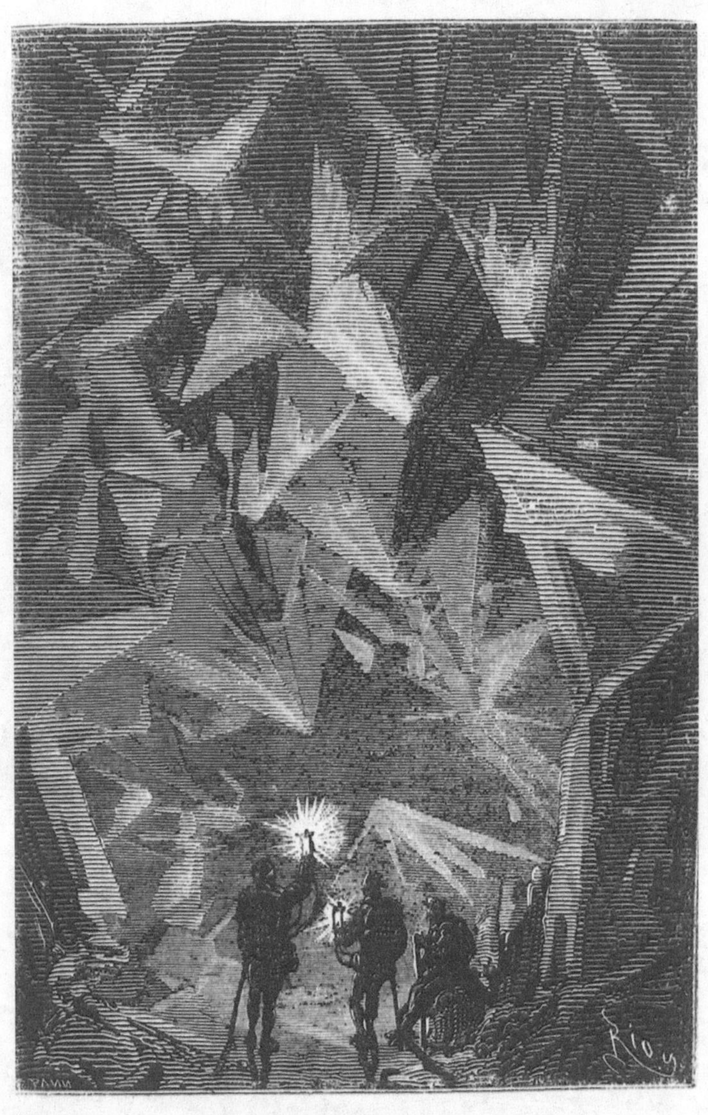

Je m'imaginais voyager à travers un diamant (p. 108).

The First Manifesto of Surrealism

14 DAYS BEFORE ANDRÉ BRETON
POET YVAN GOLL PUBLISHED
THE FIRST SURREALIST MANIFESTO

In English and French with
an essay by Martin Firrell

Cambridge
Queer Press

First published in 2024 by the Cambridge Queer Press
an imprint of MFco Ltd. Unit 4 City Limits, Danehill, Reading
RG6 4UP, UK.

ISBN 978-1-912622-50-4

Copyright © Cambridge Queer Press 2024.
www.cambridgequeerpress.co.uk

Text is set in Cormorant Garamond 13pt on 19pt.

CONTENTS

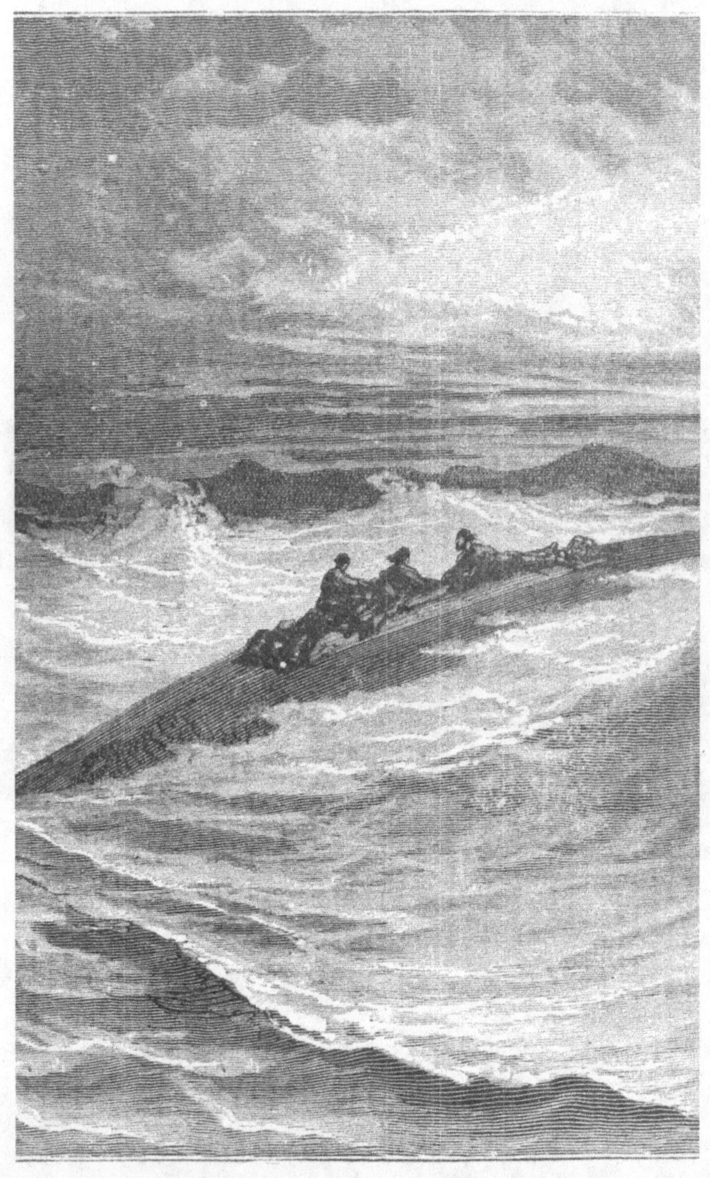

100 Years of Surrealism

Martin Firrell

At the time of writing (September 2024), the hundredth anniversary of surrealism is fast approaching. André Breton (1896-1966), regarded as the father of the surrealist movement, published *Manifeste du surréalisme* on 15th October 1924. I was under the impression it was as simple as that. And then I heard the name *Yvan Goll* for the first time. Goll (1891-1950), French-German poet, friend of famed poet Apollinaire, published his *Manifesto of Surrealism* 14 days before Breton on 1st October 1924.

I was keen to read Yvan Goll's text (published in the one and only edition of his magazine *Surréalisme*). In particular, I wanted to understand Goll's distinctive vision of surrealism and its relationship to the Bretonian variety, which emphasises the supremacy of dreams and the subconscious as source material for the surrealist poet or artist.

I was also mindful that Goll's manifesto was the movement's very first document - if only by 14 days - and to me that gave it a primacy impossible to ignore or dismiss.

It was difficult tracking down the text of Goll's manifesto. This felt ironic (or even sinister) given the overwhelming ubiquity of Breton's writings on surrealism. Eventually I found a digitised version of the Goll manifesto, in French, at Gallica, the digital library of the Bibliothèque nationale de France. As far as I could determine, there is no English translation (though it should be noted that Breton's surrealist texts are equally ubiquitous in English translation).

I set out to achieve three things: to make Yvan Goll's text available in English; to understand the ins and outs of Goll v. Breton; and, in my own way, to express creatively the spirit of Gollian surrealism, if I may call it that.

GOLL VERSUS BRETON

Yvan Goll referred to Breton's surrealism, with it reliance on chance, fantasy and dreams, as *counterfeit surrealism.*

Instead of the play of chance (most memorably summed up by the Comte de Lautréamont's line *beautiful as the chance meeting on a dissecting-table of a sewing-machine and an umbrella*) Goll called for a deeper, empirical examination of reality. He believed reality to be the substrate on which all great art rests and he advocated deepening our understanding of reality as a route to a new artform - a heightened reality or sur-realism.

FIRRELL (AFTER GOLL)

To elucidate this idea, I experimented with creating contemporary examples of Gollian surrealism in which it is the rigours of reality that dictate the juxtaposition of ideas, rather than chance or dreams. I created a poster which reads simply:

Une moule à lèvres bleues s'ouvre et révèle un cheval / A Blue-Lipped Mussel Opens and Reveals a Horse.

Whilst this may sound like a familiar 'surrealist' image, it is a million miles from Lautréamont's throw-of-the-dice on a dissecting table. This is because the juxtaposition of a mussel and a horse is based on the real (not imagined) similarity in shape

UNE MOULE
À LÈVRES
BLEUES
S'OUVRE
ET RÉVÈLE
UN CHEVAL

between a mussel shell and a horse's skull. It is an acute observation not a random association. The one leads quite practically and inexorably to the other. A close attention to the facts of reality, as demanded by Goll, is the source of this particular surrealist image.

Goll calls for a critical evaluation of the inherent nature of reality. If reality's make up can be understood more fully, it will also be possible to discern its lowest and highest forms with greater facility.

A certain type of whimsy emerges when one examines closely the underlying facts of reality as we experience it in everyday life. Goll's surrealist facts really are stranger than Breton's fiction. To illustrate this 'whimsy from fact', I created a second poster: *Lorsque la dernière orchidée sauvage est cultivée, l'orchidée sauvage n'existe plus / When the Last Wild Orchid Is Cultivated, the Wild Orchid Exists No More.*

LORSQUE
LA DERNIÈRE
ORCHIDÉE
SAUVAGE
EST CULTIVÉE,
L'ORCHIDÉE
SAUVAGE
N'EXISTE PLUS

socialart.work

The air of what could be called 'surrealist whimsy' arises from a critical assessment of the value we ascribe to a thing (in this instance, a wild flower).

We desire the wild flower because of its wild beauty, it fragility, its scarcity, its inaccessibility. But it is also a reality of human nature that when we desire something we feel compelled to possess it as completely as possible. So we grow the wild flower in a heated glasshouse in order to make it our own. We control the wild thing absolutely by bringing it under cultivation. If it then disappears from the wild (when our back is turned, as it were), though the plant itself persists, in reality, its wild form has been lost forever. That, to me, is a distinctively Gollian-surrealist grasp of reality, as profound as it is absurd, so qualifying wholeheartedly for the appellation *surrealist* as Yvan Goll saw it.

In his *Manifesto of Surrealism*, Goll uses the term *our surrealism*, presumably in contrast to the version he describes earlier in the text as *counterfeit surrealism*. These are not-so-veiled references to Breton, of course, and his alternative group of surrealists. (Breton's side boasted Louis Aragon, Robert Desnos, Paul Éluard, Jacques Baron, René Crevel, Georges Malkine, Jacques-André Boiffard and Jean Carrive and so on; Yvan Goll's side included Pierre Albert-Birot, Paul Dermée, Céline Arnauld, Francis Picabia, Tristan Tzara, Giuseppe Ungaretti, Pierre Reverdy, Marcel Arland, Joseph Delteil, Jean Painlevé and Robert Delaunay.)

Ultimately, Goll's surrealist group were willing to stop at nothing less than a profound understanding of reality's inner structure. This familiarity with the fabric and inner organisation of reality would lead, in turn, to the expression of a compelling *sur-reality*.

I created a third and final poster to explore the fruitfulness of this hypothesis: *Tout ce que je ne sais pas est inimaginable, existant dans un lieu inimaginable / Everything I Don't Know Is Unimaginable, Existing in an Unimaginable Place.*

What is unknown to the observer stands necessarily beyond their subjective reality. It is a profound truth of our quotidian lives that what we do not know, we cannot imagine. And it would be equally realistic to claim that what we cannot imagine exists in a place, which is itself beyond imagination. This strikes me as a specifically Gollian-surrealist truth. And a suitable note on which to end this short essay.

100 Years of Surrealism by public artist Martin Firrell was displayed on digital billboards throughout Belgium in partnership with Clear Channel Belgium, bringing these reflections on the nature of the surrealist movement to people from all walks of life where they live, work, play, travel and shop.

socialart.work
TOUT CE QUE
JE NE SAIS
PAS EST
INIMAGINABLE,
EXISTANT
DANS UN LIEU
INIMAGINABLE

socialart.work
TOUT CE QUE
JE NE SAIS
PAS EST
INIMAGINABLE,
EXISTANT
DANS UN LIEU
INIMAGINABLE
Clear Channel

LORSQUE
LA DERNIÈRE
ORCHIDÉE
SAUVAGE
EST CULTIVÉE,
L'ORCHIDÉE
SAUVAGE
N'EXISTE PLUS
social art work
Clear Channel

Société art work
UNE MOULE
À LÈVRES
BLEUES
S'OUVRE
ET RÉVÈLE
UN CHEVAL
Clear Channel

Manifesto of Surrealism

Yvan Goll

Reality is the basis of all great art. Without it there is no life, no substance. Reality is the ground beneath our feet and the sky above our heads.

Everything the artist creates has its starting point in nature. The cubists, in the early days, were well aware of this: as unassuming as the purest primitives, they seized on the simplest, most worthless object, going so far as to paste a piece of wallpaper, in all its reality, onto the canvas.

This transposition of reality to a higher (artistic) plane constitutes surrealism.

Guillaume Apollinaire was surrealism's driving force. If we look at his poetic work, we find the same elements as the early cubists: for him, the words of everyday life had a "strange magic", and it was with them, with the raw material of language, that he worked. Max Jacob recounts that one day Apollinaire simply jotted down phrases and words he heard in the street and turned them into a poem.

With nothing more than this basic material, he forged poetic images. These days, the image is the criterion of good poetry. The speed of association between the first impression and the final expression determines the quality of the image.

The world's first poet observed: "The sky is blue". Later, another poet noted: "Your eyes are blue like the sky". Much later, a poet went so far as to say: "You have the sky in your eyes". A contemporary poet would write: "Your eyes are sky blue". The most beautiful images are those that bring together distant elements of reality as directly and as quickly as possible.

Consequently, the image has become the most prized attribute of modern poetry. Until the beginning of the 20th Century, it was the ear that decided the quality of a poem: rhythm, sound, cadence, alliteration, rhyme: everything for the ear. For the last twenty years or so, the eye has been taking its revenge. This is the century of film. We communicate more through visual signs. And speed is the measure of quality now.

Art is a product of life, of the human being. Surrealism, as an expression of our times, reflects the qualities that characterise those times: It is direct, intense, and rejects art that relies on abstract, second-hand notions: logic, aesthetics, grammatical effects, word play.

Surrealism is more than the means of expression of one group or one country: it is international in nature, absorbing all of Europe's 'isms' and drawing on the most powerful elements in each.

Surrealism is the great movement of our times. It is sound enough, robust enough not to fall prey to the decadence that so often accompanies the emergence of new forms.

Entertainment, ballet and music-hall, curious art, picturesque art, art based on exoticism and eroticism, strange art, restless art, egotistical art, frivolous and decadent art will soon cease to amuse a generation that, after the war, needed simply to forget.

And this counterfeit surrealism, which a few ex-dadas invented to continue to impress the bourgeoisie, will soon fade from view: they assert the "omnipotence of dreams" and make

Freud a new muse. Good for Dr. Freud, using dreams to combat the world's neuroses! But to apply the same technique to the world of poetry - isn't that to confuse art with psychiatry?

Their "psychic mechanism based on dreams and the disinterested play of thought" will never be powerful enough to contradict our lived experience, which teaches us that reality is always right, that life is truer than thought.

Our surrealism returns to nature, to mankind's first and greatest love and, with completely new artistic materials, strives resolutely towards a new form, a new spirit.

Surréalisme

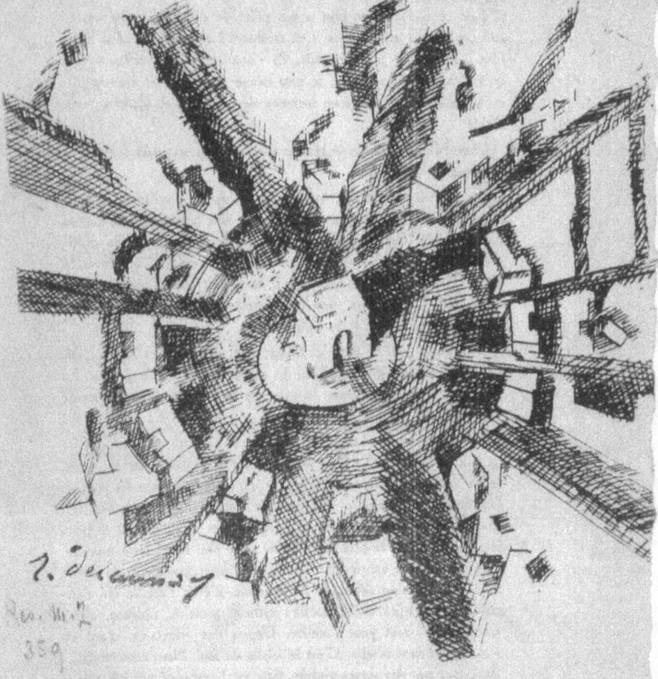

OCTOBRE 1924

1

Directeur : Ivan Goll.

Collaborateurs : Guillaume Apolli-
naire, Marcel Arland, P. Albert-
Birot, René Crevel, Joseph Delteil,
Robert Delaunay, Paul Dermée,
Jean Painlevé, Pierre Reverdy.

Manifeste du surréalisme

Yvan Goll

La réalité est la base de tout grand art. Sans elle pas de vie, pas de substance. La réalité, c'est le sol sous nos pieds et le ciel sur notre tête.

Tout ce que l'artiste crée a son point de départ dans la nature. Les cubistes, à leurs débuts, s'en rendirent bien compte: aussi humbles que les plus purs primitifs, ils s'abaissèrent profondément jusqu'à l'objet le plus simple, le plus dénué de valeur, et allèrent jusqu'à coller sur le tableau un morceau de papier peint, dans toute sa réalité.

Cette transposition de la réalité dans un plan

supérieur (artistique) constitue le Surréalisme.

Le surréalisme est une conception qu'anima Guillaume Apollinaire. En examinant son œuvre poétique, nous y trouvons les mêmes éléments que chez les premiers cubistes: les mots de la vie quotidienne ont pour lui « une magie étrange », et c'est avec eux, avec la matière première du langage, qu'il travaillait. Max Jacob raconte qu'un jour, Apollinaire nota simplement des phrases et des mots entendus dans la rue, et en fit un poème.

Seulement avec ce matériel élémentaire, il forma des images poétiques. L'image est aujourd'hui le critère de la bonne poésie. La rapidité d'association entre la première impression et la dernière expression fait la qualité de l'image.

Le premier poète au monde constata: « Le ciel est bleu ». Plus tard, un autre trouva: « Tes yeux sont bleus comme le ciel ». Longtemps après, on se hasarda à dire: « Tu as du ciel dans les yeux ». Un moderne s'écriera: « Tes yeux de ciel ! ». Les plus belles images sont celles qui rapprochent des éléments de la réalité éloignés les uns des autres le plus directement et le plus rapidement possible.

Ainsi, l'image est devenue l'attribut le plus apprécié de la poésie moderne. jusqu'au début du XXᵉ siècle, c'était l'oreille qui décidait de la qualité d une poésie: rythme, sonorité, cadence, allitération, rime: tout pour l oreille. Depuis une vingtaine d'années, l'œil prend sa revanche. C'est le siècle du film. Nous communiquons davantage par des signes visuels. Et c'est la rapidité qui fait aujourd'hui la qualité.

L'art est une émanation de la vie et de l'organisme de l'homme. Le surréalisme, expression de notre époque, tient compte des symptômes qui la caractérisent: il est direct, intensif, et il repousse les arts qui s'appuient sur des notions abstraites et de seconde main : logique, esthétique, effets de grammaire, jeux de mots.

Le surréalisme ne se contente pas d'être le

moyen d'expression d'un groupe ou d'un pays: il
sera international, il absorbera tous les ismes qui
partagent l'Europe, et recueillera les éléments
vitaux de chacun.

Le surréalisme est un vaste mouvement de
l'époque. Il signifie la santé, et repoussera aisément
les tendances de décomposition et de morbidité qui
surgissent partout où quelque chose se construit.

L'art de divertissement, l'art des ballets et du
music-hall, l'art curieux, l'art pittoresque, l'art à
base d'exotisme et d'érotisme, l'art étrange, l'art
inquiet, l'art égoïste, l'art frivole et décadent
auront bientôt cessé d'amuser une génération qui,
après la guerre, avait besoin d'oublier.

Et cette contrefaçon du surréalisme, que
quelques ex-dadas ont inventée pour continuer
à épater les bourgeois, sera vite mise hors de
la circulation:

Ils affirment la « toute-puissance du rêve » et
font de Freud une muse nouvelle. Que le docteur

Freud se serve du rêve pour guérir des troubles
trop terrestres, fort bien! Mais de là à faire de sa
doctrine une application dans le monde poétique,
n'est-ce pas confondre art et psychiâtrie?

Leur « mécanisme psychique basé sur le rêve
et le jeu désintéressé de la pensée » ne sera jamais
assez puissant pour ruiner notre organisme
physique qui nous enseigne que la réalité a
toujours raison, que la vie est plus vraie que
la pensée.

Notre surréalisme retrouve la nature,
l'émotion première de l'homme, et va, avec un
matériel artistique complètement neuf, vers une
construction, vers une volonté.

Cambridge
Queer Press